Dedicated to my parents

Without whose support this book would have been far from completion

Acknowledgement

No creation in this world is a solo effort. Neither is this book. From the person who makes copies of the draft to the delivery boy who makes them reach shops, everyone has a role. I would like to thank all those whose contributions have been significant in shaping me.

Firstly, I'd like to thank my readers because of whom I am who I am. Secondly, I'd like to thank my family members, friends', professors and all those entrepreneurs whose views have been a guiding light in my journey. Last but not the least, I'd like to make a special mention about AIESEC in Chennai for helping me develop my skill set.

TABLE OF CONTENT

Chapter 1: Considerations to Make

Before getting started, please ask yourself

Are you a budding entrepreneur? Do you want your startup to be a success?

If yes, then here are some of the aspects that you should consider:

1) Foresight
  - Socioeconomic trends
  - Societal and cultural trends
  - regulatory trends
  - technology trends

2) Market Analysis
  - market segments
  - needs and demands
  - market issues
  - switching costs
  - revenue attractiveness

3) Industry Forces
  - suppliers and other value chain actors
  - stakeholders
  - competitors(incumbents)

> new entrants(insurgents)
> substitute products and services

4) Macro Economics

> global market conditions
> capital markets
> commodities and other resources
> economic infrastructure

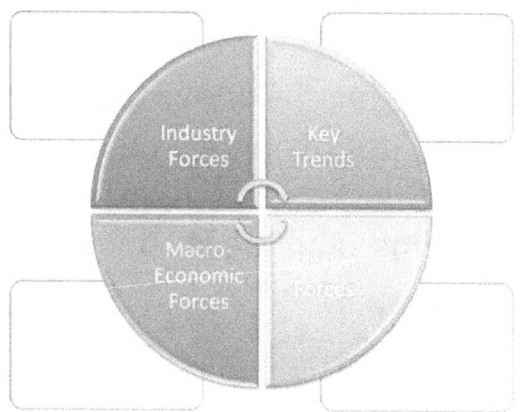

A competitive business model that makes sense in today's environment might be outdated tomorrow. We have to improve our understanding of a model's environment and how it might evolve so as to sustain in the market. Of course we can't be certain about the future, because of the complexities and uncertainties, involved in the evolving business environment. We can, however, develop a number of hypotheses about the future to serve as guidelines for designing tomorrow's business models. Assumptions about how market forces, industry forces, key trends, and macroeconomic forces are important considerations as they give us an idea on how to develop potential business model options or prototypes for the future.

Okay after taking the above considerations into account, following next are a list of four essential techniques that you should apply before Moving onto the Business model canvassing

Chapter 2: Business Model Design Techniques

Business Model Design Techniques

- Customer Perspective
- Ideation
- Visual Thinking
- Prototyping

Customer Centric Business model - Know your customers

Most businesses don't take into account the customer perspectives. They are centered around the organization. Answering questions such as-

What can we sell to customers?
How can we reach customers most efficiently?
What relationships do we need to establish with customers?
How can we make money from our customers?

Adopting the customer profiling is a guiding principle for a successful business model design. It involves looking at a product or venture from the point of view of the customer. For your business model to be customer centric ask yourself these basic questions

What job(s) do (es) my customer need to get done and how can I help?
What are our customer's aspirations and how can I help him live up to them?
How does my customers prefer to be addressed?
How do we, as an enterprise, best fit into their routines?
What relationship do my customers expect us to establish with them?
For what value(s) are customers truly willing to pay?

An example of this type of model is Apple's iPod media player. Apple perceived that consumers wanted a seamless way to search, download, and listen to digital content, including music, and were willing to pay for a successful solution. Apple's view was unique at a time when illegal downloading was rampant and most companies argued that nobody would be willing to pay for digital music online Apple dismissed these views and created a seamless music experience for customers, integrating the iTunes music and media software, the iTunes online store, and the iPod media player. With this Value Proposition as the crust of its business model, Apple went on to dominate the online digital music market.

Apple iPod/iTunes Business Model Canvas

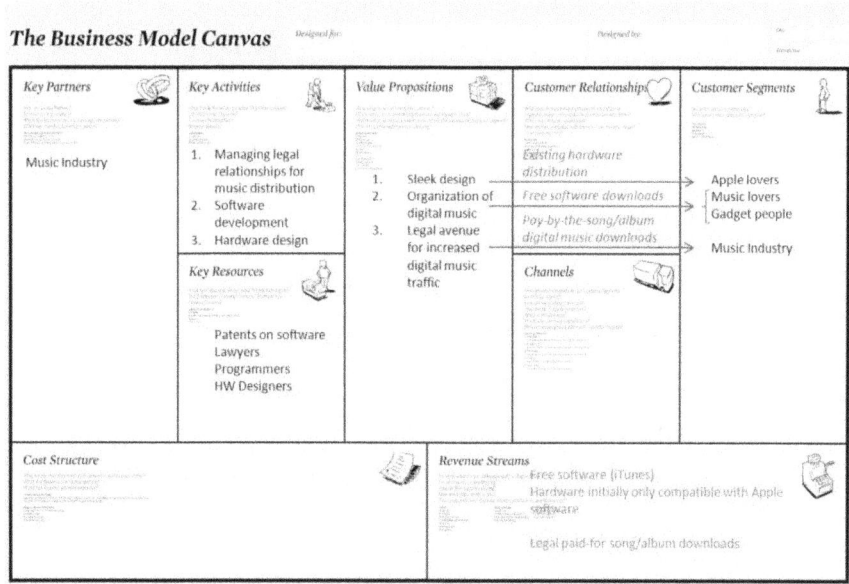

Note: Just pay a cursory look at the other figure and come back to it after the subsequent chapter

Ideation:

To come up with new or better options, you must think of a bag full of ideas before narrowing them down to a short list of conceivable options. Thus, ideation has two main phases: idea generation, where quantity matters, and synthesis, in which ideas are discussed, combined, and narrowed down to a small number of viable options.

Business model innovation is not about looking back, because the past indicates little about what is possible in terms of future business models. Business model innovation is not about looking to competitors, since business model innovation is not about copying or benchmarking, but about creating new mechanisms to create value and derive revenues.

Epicenters for ideations:
Innovative ideas for business models can originate from any one of the nine blocks (to be discussed later on) but they are of the general 2 types:

1) Resource driven: These ideas come from the available existing resources or partnerships with the organization, to expand or transform the organization.
2) Offer driven: These innovations are a result of modification of the business value propositions that in turn affects other blocks.

Visualization:

Write ideas down or sketch them out on a surface everyone can see. A good way to collect ideas is to jot them down on Post-it™ notes and stick these to a wall. This allows you to move ideas around and also makes it easier to group them. Post-it™ notes:

Drawings:

Drawings can be even more powerful than Post-it™ notes because people Re-act more strongly to images than to words. Pictures deliver messages instantly and as rightly said a picture is worth a thousand words.

A common misconception is that one shouldn't draw something until one understands it. Its the contrary, sketches—however rudimentary or amateurish—help people better describe, discuss and understand issues, particularly those of a complex nature.

The problem is that most of us think that we can't draw or are shy to draw lest someone makes fun of us for our childish drawing, but the truth is that even crude drawings, sincerely rendered, make things tangible and understandable. For example: A stick figure with a smiling face conveys a positive emotion.
A big bag of money and a small bag of money convey proportions. Such drawings will likely trigger constructive discussion

from which new business model ideas will emerge.

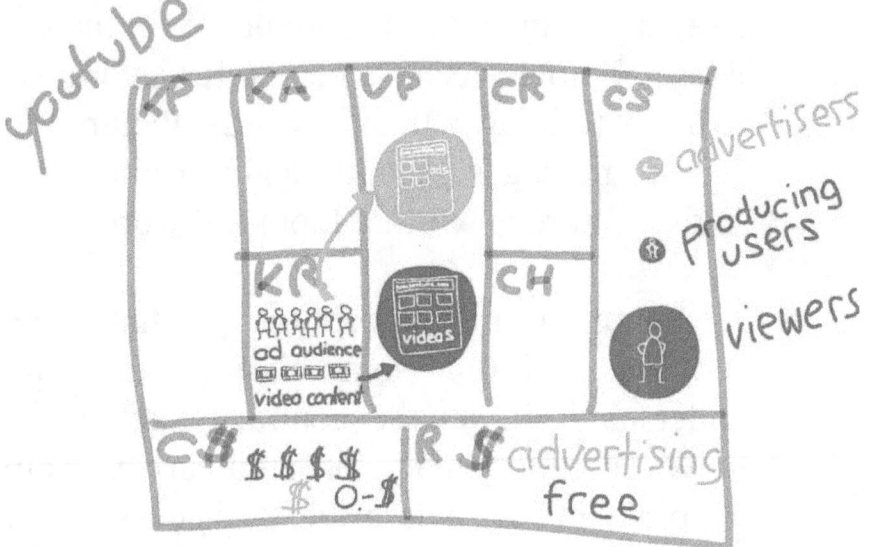

Even something this rudimentary is sufficient to convey the message across

Advantages:
Easier visualization
Understanding the essence
Enhance Dialogue
Explore Ideas
Improves Communication

Prototyping:

Prototyping comes from the design and engineering disciplines, where it is widely used for product design and architecture. A business model prototype can take the form of a simple sketch, a fully thought-through concept described either with the Business Model Canvas or a spreadsheet that simulates the financial workings of a new business. Not only does it give us a general outlook of a business model will look like but tells us in detail of how changing one parameter affects the rest of the business. For example how does the model change if we add another client segment? What are the consequences of removing a costly resource? What if we gave away something for free and replaced that Revenue Stream with something more innovative? And so on.

To be at the top you need to emphasize on prototyping, open your mind to new ideas, making small changes and open yourself to value and efficiency focused opportunistic thinking. As both inside and outside business models transform industries. Business model prototypes vary in terms of scale and level of refinement. Apart from playing a role in pre-implementation visualization and testing they also serve as a tool of enquiry that aids in exploration of new possibilities.

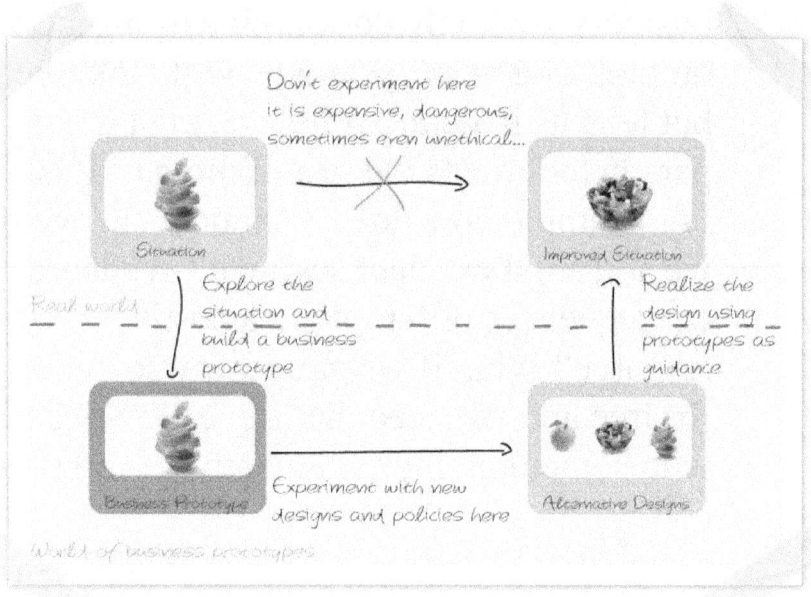

 As rightly said by Jim Glymph, Gehry Partners "If you freeze an idea too quickly, you fall in love with it. If you refine it too quickly, you become attached to it and it becomes very hard to keep exploring, to keep looking for better. The crudeness of the early models in particular is very deliberate."

Chapter 3: Business Model Canvas

Now that we have seen the various designing techniques and considerations, let's begin with the real deal
Business Model Canvas:

It consists primarily 9 blocks –

1) Customer Segments
2) Value Propositions
3) Value Propositions
4) Customer Relationships
5) Revenue Streams
6) Key Resources
7) Key Activities
8) Key Partnerships
9) Cost Structure

1) **Customer Segment:**

It refers to the group or class of people you target to sell your product or offer service to. Customers comprise the heart of any business model. Without (profitable)

customers, no company can survive for long. In order to better satisfy customers, a company may group them into distinct segments with respect to needs, liking, desire, purchase power or other attributes.

A business model may define one or several large or small Customer Segments. An organization must choose which segments to serve and which segments to ignore due to the versatility of need and demands of different groups. Once this decision is made, a business model can be carefully designed around a strong understanding of specific customer needs.

Customer groups represent separate segments if:

• *Their needs and requirements vary*
• *They are reached through different Distribution Channels*
• *They require different types of relationships*
• *They have substantially different earning capabilities*

The different types of customer segments are :

Mass market – This type of market consists of one large group of people with similar problems and needs. The value Propositions, Distribution Channels and Customer Relationships are all focused on this large group. The business models of this type don't differentiate between various customer Segments. Example: Coca-Cola, an aerated drink that is consumed by all people alike.

KEY PARTNERS	KEY ACTIV...		VALUE PROPOSITION	CUSTOMER RELATIONSHIPS		CUSTOMER SEGMENTS
	Bottling	Distribution		Displays and fridges	Advertiseme nt to consumers	
Sabco (bottler)	Producing and supply syrup	Marketing		Resident account developer (RAD)		Larger retail outlets
	KEY RESOURCES			CHANNELS		
Manual Distribution Centre Owners	Secret recipe	Bottling plant and distribution center		Large scale distribution		Small shops/ restaurants
	Syrup Factory	Bottles and Crates			Manual Distribution Centers	
COST STRUCTURE				REVENUE STREAMS		
Marketing	Producing syrup	Bottling and distribution		Bulk sales		Retail price/ crate (- fixed margin for MDC)

Example of a mass market

Niche market – This type of market cater to specific Customer Segments. The Value Propositions, Distribution Channels, and Customer Relationships are all tailored to the specific requirements of a niche market. Such markets require accurate knowledge of the markets scenario and the target audience. For example: many of the bike parts are specific to that particular bike or manufacturer.

Example of a Niche market, depicted in blue

Segmented – Some businesses differentiate between markets which have slightly varying demands and problems. An example of this type is SBI, State Bank of India which may have a different approach of contacting, credit limit and serviceability for persons with annual income above 10 lakhs rupees and those with incomes above 20 lakhs rupees

Example of segmented market, where the same color circles denote same segments

Diversified - An organization which serves two or more unrelated Customer Segments with very different needs and problems is said to have a diversified customer business model.

Multi-sided markets- An organization serving two or more interdependent Customer Segments is said to be a multi-sided organization. For example, TATA which manufactures salt, cars, trucks, own tea and Coffee plantations, generates power, electronic store, constructs houses and owns much more. Another example is Metro, an enterprise offering a free newspaper needs a large reader base to attract advertisers. On the other hand, it also needs advertisers to finance production and distribution. Both segments are required to make the business model work successfully.

Various TATA products

2) **Value Proposition:**

The Value Propositions Building Block describes the bundle of products and services that create value for a specific Customer Segment through a distinct mix of elements catering to that segment's needs. Value Proposition is the reason why a customer gives preference to a company over the other. It either solves a customer's problem or satisfies his demand.

Values may be quantitative (e.g. price, speed of service) or qualitative (e.g. design, customer experience).Some value propositions may be new and unique while they others may be similar to existing ones but with added features

While designing the Value Proposition ask yourself the following questions:

What value do I deliver to the customer?
Which one of my customer's problems am I helping to solve?
Which customer segments am I satisfying?
What bundles of products and services am I offering to each Customer Segment?

technologies, or a combination of both. Example: Franchising of Starbucks in India

Convenience/usability- Improvement of usability or convenience of use tends to improve the user friendliness of the product thereby increasing sales. Example: the development of various apps in different OS leading to increase in productivity and easy usability.

3) Channels

They are the Building Block which describe how a company communicates with and reaches its Customer Segments to deliver a Value Proposition. Communication, distribution, and sales Channels constitute the interface of a company with its customers. Channels play an important role in the customer experience.

Channels serve several functions, including:

• Create awareness among customers about a company's products and services
• Helping customers assess a company's Value Proposition
• Facilitate customers to buy specific products and services
• Delivering a Value Proposition to customers
• Providing post-purchase customer service and support

Again, before we move on to the factors affecting channeling decisions, ask yourself the following questions.

Which Channel works best for the customer or how they want to be reached?
How am I reaching them now?
How are my Channels integrated with customer routines?
Which channels are most cost-efficient for me?

Facebook – World's leading Social Networking Site (SNS)				
Key Partners	**Key Activities**	**Value Propositions**	**Relationships**	**Customer Segments**
Content Partners (TV Shows, Movies, Music, News Articles)	Platform Development	Connect with your friends, Discover & Learn, Express yourself	Same-side Network Effects	Internet Users
	Data Center Operations Mgmt		Cross-side Network Effects	
	Key Resources	Reach, Relevance, Social Context, Engagement		Advertisers and Marketers
	Facebook Platform		**Channels**	
		Personalized and Social Experiences, Social Distribution, Payments	Website, Mobile Apps	Developers
	Technology Infrastructure		Facebook Ads, Facebook Pages	
			Developer Tools and APIs	

Cost Structure			**Revenue Streams**		
Data center costs	Marketing and Sales	Research and Development	Free	Ad Revenues	Payment Revenues
General and Administrative					

Example: Business model canvas of Facebook, depicting various channels used

The various types of channeling are:

Sales force – It a direct method of sales where the business itself takes up the responsibility to sell its products or services. Example: Kent R.O water purifiers

Web sales – Online media and advertising is used here. It can de both direct viz. done by the company or indirect viz. outsourcing of an advertising agency. Example: sale of Redme phones

Own stores- It involves the company selling its product by setting out an outlet, generally having higher margins, but can be costly to put in place and to operate. Example: Bata, a shoe store sets up its factory outlet

Partner stores - It is an indirect method of sales wherein a company has a tie up with other outlets to facilitate sale of their product through their stores. Example: Pantaloons outlets sell Clothing of other brands as well. Partner Channels lead to lower margins, but they allow an organization to expand its reach and benefit from partner strengths

Wholesaler – At wholesaler the products are sold in bulk quantities, generally their customers are the retailers. Example: Metro shopping in Bengaluru.
The trick is to find the right balance between the different types of Channels, to integrate them in a way to improve customer experience, and to maximize revenues.

Ponder over the various phases of channeling, which are:

Awareness
How do we create awareness about our company's products and services?

Assessment
How do we help customers assess our organization's Value Proposition?

Purchase
How do we allow customers to purchase specific products and services?

Delivery
How do we deliver a Value Proposition to customers?

After sales
How do we provide post-purchase customer support?

4) Customer Relationships:

The Customer Relationships Building Block describes the types of relationships a company establishes with specific Customer Segments. A company should be specific about the type of relationship it wants to maintain with each Customer Segment. Relationships can range from personal to automatic.

Customer relationships are driven by the following motivations:

• Customer acquisition
• Customer retention
• Boosting sales to existing customer

Example: In the earlier days the cellular networks main intention was to acquire users while now, due to increase in competition, their motto is to retain them.

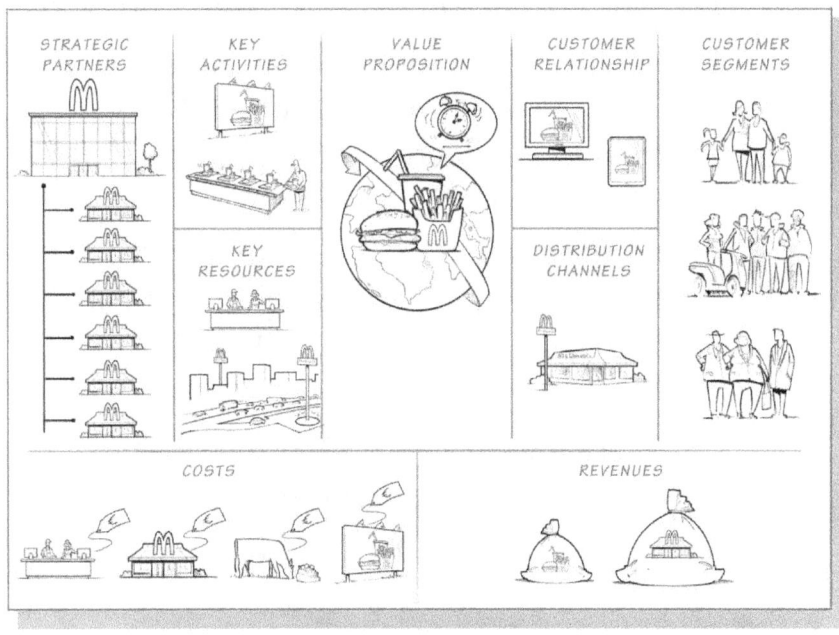

Example: Business model canvas of McDonalds, depicting its customer relations

The various types of customer relations are:

Personal assistance - The customers can communicate with a customer representative to get help during the sales process or after sales period. This may happen onsite at the point of sale, through call centers or by e-mail.

Dedicated personal assistance - involves assigning a customer representative specifically to an individual client. It represents the deepest and most intimate type of relationship and normally develops over a long period of time. In private banking services, for example, dedicated bankers serve high net worth individuals

Self-service- in this type of relation no personal contact is maintained, all means and tools for help are to be taken care of by the customer himself.

Automated services – This type of relationship is a more advanced form of self-service where in the customer is provided all the tools to help himself online. The systems are capable of recognizing the customer from his username and specific help can be provided. Example: crashing of a computer software, say vlc player, the problem is diagnosed and help is received online.

Communities- Similar to self-help, but communities facilitate discussion by a group of people about a problem and its solution.

The communities are increasing in number and size. Example: RC cars help community to discuss strategies, problems, parts and settings used for RC cars.

Co-creation- More companies are going beyond the traditional customer-vendor relationship to co-create value with customers. Flipkart.com invites customers to write reviews about products and thus create value for other users as well.
Some companies engage customers to assist with the design of new and innovative products.

Now, before selecting the type of customer relation, ask yourself:

What type of relationship does each of our Customer Segments expect us to establish and maintain with them?
Which ones have I established?
How costly are they? How can I minimize the cost incurred?

5) Revenue Streams:

The Revenue Streams Building Block represents the cash a company generates from each Customer Segment. If customers comprise the heart of a business model, Revenue Streams are its arteries.

The following are the questions a company must ask itself:

For what value is each Customer Segment truly willing to pay?

Successfully answering that question allows the firm to generate one or more Revenue Streams from each Customer Segment. Each Revenue Stream may have different pricing mechanisms, such as fixed list prices, bargaining, auctioning, market dependent, volume dependent, or yield management.

Revenue systems can be classified into two main categories:

- Depending on the **method of payment-**

- **Transaction revenue** resulting from one-time payment
- **Recurring revenue** resulting from continuous service or purchase.

- Depending on the **type of payment-**

  - **Fixed Pricing -** involves the product being sold at the same price with less or no variation. The Price is a function of the quantity of items sold
  - **Dynamic pricing-** A product or service whose price changes with availability and demand is said to be dynamically

priced. This is generally the case with perishable goods.

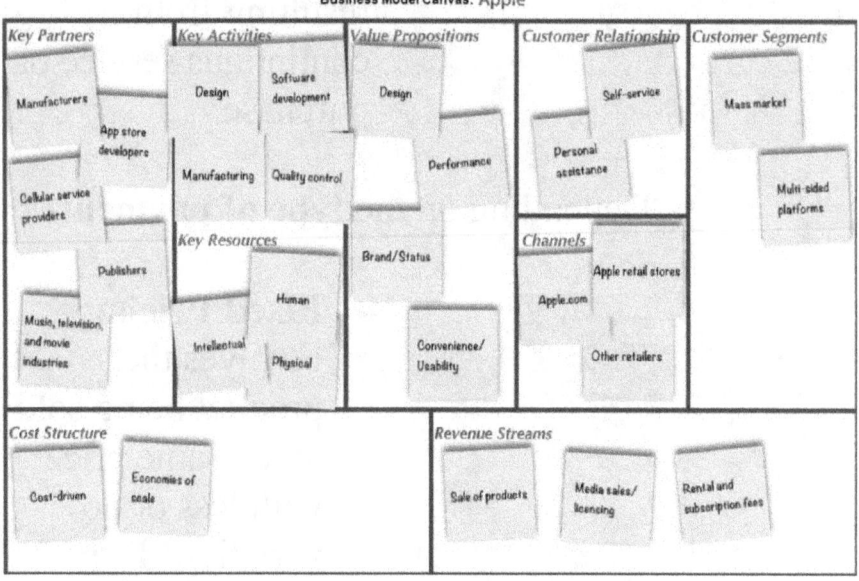

Business Model Canvas: Apple

Example: Revenue Streams for Apple

The following are the ways to generate revenue streams:

Usage fee- The amount payable by a customer is proportional to the usage. Example, a telecom operator may charge customers for the number of minutes spent on the phone. A transporter charges customers for the distance through which the goods are to be transferred.

Subscription fees- This Revenue Stream is generated by selling continuous access to a service. Some examples are Nokia's Comes with Music service gives users access to a music library for a subscription fee. WhatsApp comes at a nominal subscription of rupees 55 (1$) a year. A swimming pool offers to its member's monthly or yearly subscriptions in exchange for access to its pool facilities.

Asset sale- involves selling ownership rights to a physical product. Example: flipkart.com sells books, music, consumer electronics, and more online. Ford sells automobiles, which buyers are free to drive, resell, or even destroy.

Lending/Renting/Leasing – here a product or service is rendered to customer for a specific time period after which the customer has a choice whether to continue with the deal or to discard it. Example: INS

Vikrant, a carrier ship of India is leased from Russia for every 10 years.

Licensing- Here a company can lend its intellectual property for other customers or companies to use at a fees charged from them for the same. The company retains a copy right or patent copy with itself to prevent unauthorized usage of its property. Example: Any product requiring a product/ License key, example Office 2014, so on.

Brokerage fees- This type of Revenue System involves a sort of matching fees collectable on the matching of a buyer and a seller from among two or more parties. Example A real estate agent matching buyers and sellers or owners to tenants.

Advertising - This Revenue Stream results from fees for advertising a particular product, service, or brand. It can be done via media industry, event managers or even via online media, depending on the reach needed and budget constraints present.

6) **Key Resources:**

The Key Resources Building Block describes the most important assets required to make a business model work. These resources allow enterprises to create and offer a Value Proposition, cover markets, maintain relationships with Customer Segments, and earn revenues.

The Key Resources needed vary depending upon the type of business model. A computer hardware's manufacturer requires capital-intensive production facilities, whereas a computer software's designer focuses more on human resources. Key resources can be physical, financial, intellectual, or human. Key resources can be owned or leased by the company or acquired from key partners.

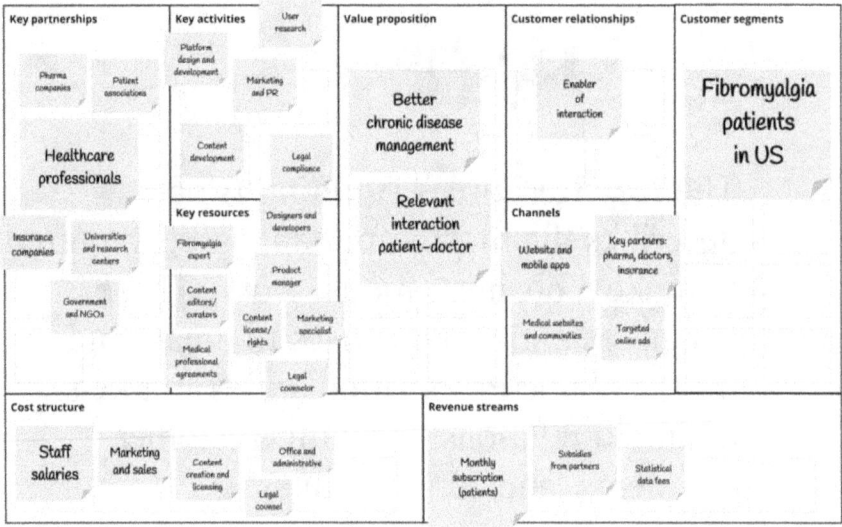

Dobby

Key partnerships

Pharma companies

Patient associations

Healthcare professionals

Insurance companies

Universities and research centers

Government and NGOs

Key activities

Platform design and development

Marketing and PR

Content development

Legal compliance

User research

Key resources

Fibromyalgia expert

Content editors/curators

Medical professional agreements

Designers and developers

Product manager

Content license/rights

Marketing specialist

Legal counselor

Value proposition

Better chronic disease management

Relevant interaction patient-doctor

Customer relationships

Enabler of interaction

Channels

Website and mobile apps

Key partners: pharma, doctors, insurance

Medical websites and communities

Targeted online ads

Customer segments

Fibromyalgia patients in US

Cost structure

Staff salaries

Marketing and sales

Content creation and licensing

Office and administrative

Legal counsel

Revenue streams

Monthly subscription (patients)

Subsidies from partners

Statistical data fees

Example: Business model canvas of Dobby, the American healthcare giant, depicts its vast key resources

Key resources are of the following types-

Physical- This category consists of physical assets such as manufacturing facilities, buildings, vehicles, machines, systems, point-of-sales systems, and distribution networks. Manufacturers like Honda and retailers like Amazon.com rely heavily on physical resources, which are often capital-intensive. The former has an enormous global network of sales and manufacturing. The latter has an extensive IT, warehouse, and logistics infrastructure.

Intellectual- This category consists of resources such as partnerships, proprietary, patents and copyrights, knowledge, brands and customer databases are important components of a strong business model. Intellectual resources are difficult to develop but when successfully created may offer a substantial value. Example: Intel, a designer and supplier of chipsets for electronic devices such as computers, laptops and phones, built its business model around patented microchip designs that earn the company a substantial licensing fees.

Human- Every company requires human resources, but people are particularly prominent in certain business models. For example: In technological firms number of employees depicts the work force , thus the strength of the company and leads to more deals being made with that company.

Financial- Some models require financial resources and/or financial guarantees, such as cash, lines of credit, or a stock option pool for hiring key employees. Example: most banking sectors are expected to keep a base percentage of their total monetary resources with the RBI, Reserve Bank of India to function smoothly.

Now that we have seen the different key resources decide on what your startup need by individually answering:

What Key Resources do your Value Propositions, Distribution Channels, Customer Relationships and Revenue Streams require?

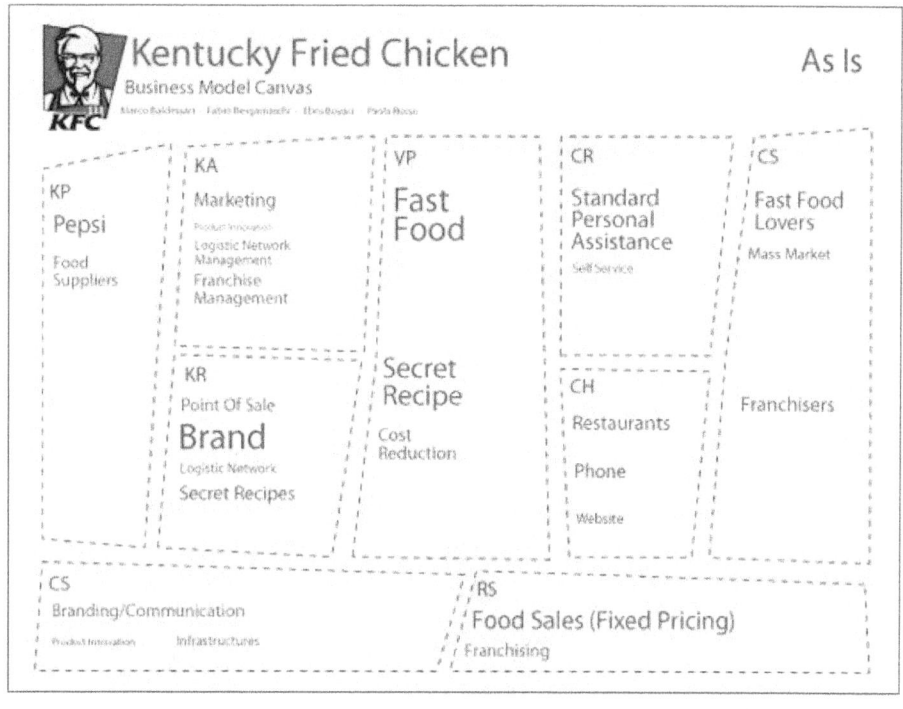

Example: Key Resources of Kentucky's Fried Chicken

7) **Key Activities:**

The Key Activities Building Block describes the most important things a company must do in order to ensure its business model work. It involves planning all the set of actions to be taken by the company for the business to move forward. Like Key Resources, they vary depending on the business type and are required to create and offer a Value Proposition, reach markets, maintain Customer Relationships, and earn revenues. Example: For Phone manufacturer Nokia, Key Activities include supply chain management. For consultancy TCS, Tata Consultancy Services Key Activities include software assistance and problem solving.

Key activities can be as follows:

Production - These activities involve the designing, manufacturing and delivery of a product in substantial quality and quantities.

Problem solving- The Key Activities involved here relate to providing new solutions to individual customer problems. The operations of consultancies, hospitals, and other service organizations are typically dominated by problem solving activities. Their business models call for activities such as knowledge management and continuous training.

Platform/network- The Key Activities involved here are network or platform related. Creating and managing a network of Platform for business transactions and data transfer to take place.
 Example: Visa's business model requires activities related to its Visa® credit card transaction platform for merchants, customers, and banks. Apple's business model requires managing the interface between other vendors' software and its Mac® operating system platform.

Key Partners	Key Activities	Value Propositions	Relationships	Customer Segments
	Payments Network Management	Payment Product Platforms for card programs and cashless payments		Financial Institutions (Issuers)
Technology Alliances	Transaction Processing			Financial Institutions (Acquirers)
	Value-added Services			
Commercial Partners	**Key Resources**	Convenience, Security, Rewards associated with card payments	**Channels**	Card Holders
	Payment Products Platform		Sponsorships (FIFA World cup, Olympics)	
	VISA Brand	Improved Sales, Customer Convenience	TV ads, Tradeshows, Conferences	Merchants

Cost Structure			Revenue Streams		
Personnel	Network, EDP, & Communications	Brand Promotion	Services Revenues	Data Processing Revenues	International Revenues
Litigations Provision					

Example: Business model canvas of VISA, showing the key activities it undertakes

Now. Think about:
The key Activities that I should undertake?
What is the demand and competition in the activities I am performing?

8) **Key Partnerships:**

The Key Partnerships Building Block describes the network of producers, suppliers and partners that make the business model work. The key partnerships can be the backbone of the organization. There are four types of partnerships namely,

- Strategic alliances between non-competitors
- Coopetition: strategic partnerships between competitors
- Joint ventures to develop new businesses
- Buyer-supplier relationships to assure reliable supplies

Before we move onto the motives behind partnerships, stop and ponder over these:

- Who are my Key Partners?
- Who are my key suppliers?
- Which Key Resources am I acquiring from partners?
- Which Key Activities do my partners perform?

Now, moving on to the motives behind partnerships:

Reduction of risk/ uncertainty- All organizations prefer to have low risks involved and to have a high level of market certainty, but this is not the situation in most cases. So, this leads an organization to partner with other firms to share the risk involved thereby reducing risks. Example: Initial partnership between Maruti, an Indian government enterprise and Suzuki, a Japanese motor company to give Maruti Suzuki, while now the company is completely owned by Suzuki.

Optimization of economy- It is a rarity for a company to own all resources or perform every activity by itself. Hence, most companies combine their resources to increase their pool of funds, reduce costs and share infrastructures. Example, the 70-30 partnership between Reliance banking and SBI, State Bank of India.

Acquisition of resources and activities- Even though a company may possess all the resources it needs to perform the activities listed in its business model it may prefer to outsource other companies dealing with specific aspects of the work, plausibly due to the need to acquire knowledge, licenses, or access to customers. Taking the above example, the reason Reliance banking partnered 30% with the SBI is because of the national presence that the SBI has, making it easier to serve a larger base of customers.

Business Model of Banking companies

Key Partners	Key Activities	Value Propositions	Relationships	Customer Segments
Investments partners	Branch Operations		Personal Assistance	
	Call center operations	Deposit Products (Lower Interest Rates)	Automation where possible	Retail and Corporate Customers (Depositors)
Technology vendors	IT Operations			
Regulatory Agencies	**Key Resources**	Loan Products (Higher Interest Rates)	**Channels**	Retail and Corporate Customers (Borrowers)
	Physical and IT Infrastructure		Bank Branches, ATMs, Call centers, Internet, Mobile Devices	
	Loan Assets			

Cost Structure		Revenue Streams	
Interest Expenses	Channel Costs	Interest Income	Fee Income

9) Cost Structure:

The Cost Structure describes all the costs incurred during the operation of a business. Creating and delivering value, managing Customer Relationships, and generating revenue all incur costs. Such costs can be calculated relatively easily after defining Key Resources, Key Activities, and Key Partnerships. The objective of any business is to minimize costs and maximize profits. The Cost Structure block is an important classification factor between cost driven and value driven businesses.

The two extremes:

Cost Driven structure- The main motto of these type of companies is to minimize costs while not adversely affecting the quality. They tend to maximize their profits by offering a low cost value proposition thereby rely on the quantity to maximize profits. Maximize automation minimize outsourcing are two techniques employed here. Example:

the Air Conditioning unit in a BMW costs rupees 50,000(approx. 1000 $) while a similar one developed by Nissan costs only rupees 3500(approx. 70 $).

Value Driven structure- Some companies are less concerned about the cost and are more focused on the quality of product or service they supply. Generally luxury products or services come into this category. Example: Luxury hotels and resorts, with their lavish facilities and exquisite services, fall into this category.

Characteristics of Cost Driven structures are:

Fixed Costs- Here the cost remains the same in spite of the varying volume of goods or services produced. Examples include salaries and rents. Some businesses, such as manufacturing companies, are characterized by a high proportion of fixed costs.

Variable Costs- Costs that vary in proportion to the volume of goods or services produced. Some businesses, such as Transportation or packaging industry, are characterized by a high proportion of variable costs.

Scale Economies- Cost advantages that a business enjoys as its output expands. For example a larger company will have a lower cost per unit due to bulk order or production, whichever the case may be, this and other factors cause average cost per unit to fall.

Scope Economies- Cost advantages that a business enjoys due to a larger scope of operations. For example between a toy company which manufactures ten toys and a toy manufacturing company which manufactures only one toy, it would be easier for the former to manufacture a new toy over the latter, due to the availability of varied manufacturing tools and as well as their wide base marketing activities or Distribution Channels may support multiple products for the pre-established company.

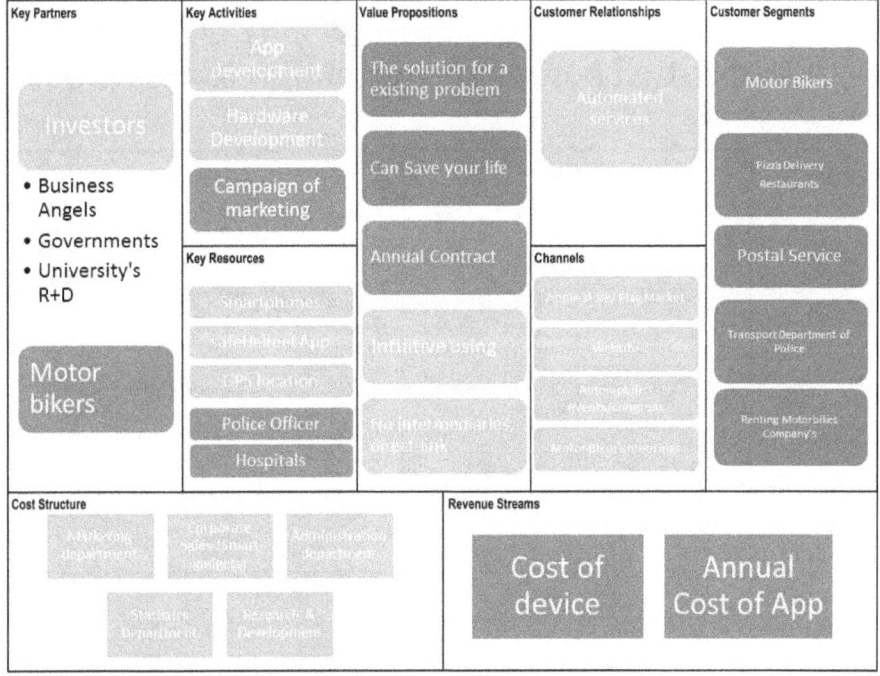

Example: For cost structure of a Helmet manufacturing company

Now integrating all that has been covered by the 9 blocks we get what is known as
Business Model Canvas

The template has been given below, go ahead and fill it. Get as many ideas as possible even the ones that seem too crazy, write them down, because there is no harm in trying. Also mistakes, if any are most welcome, but at this stage only and must be rectified before execution of business model.

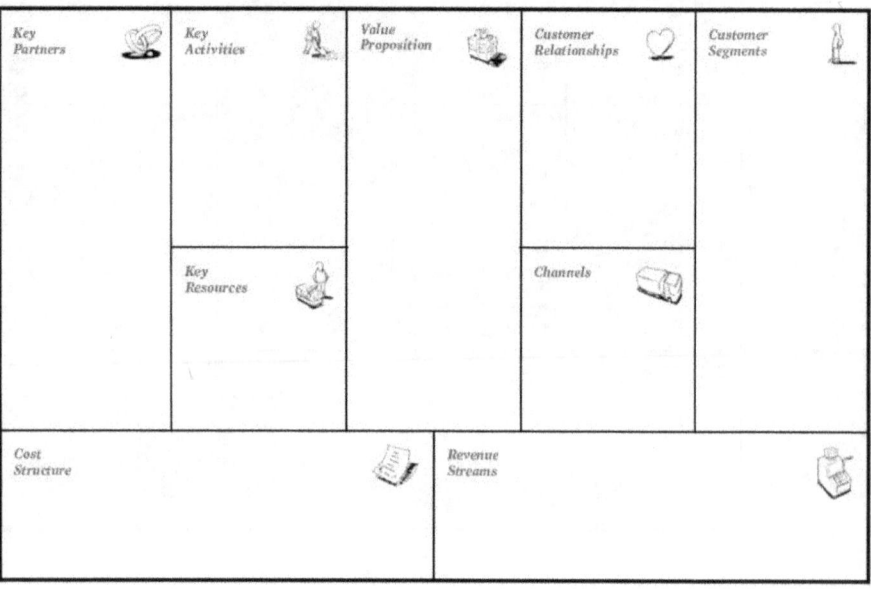

Hoping that by now, you have created your Business model. If yes, then it is great. Now it is time to assess how feasible your plan is, here we will use a Technique known as SWOT.

Chapter 4: SWOT

It stands for Strength, Weakness, Opportunity and Threats. As the name suggest, it is an assessment of your organizations strength, weakness, opportunity and threats. It is an attractive tool because of its simplicity, yet its use can lead to vague discussions because of the uncertainty on what factors should be preferred over the other. Hence, to partly solve this problem in the questionnaire below there is a table where weights of numerical values of the factors can be entered beside them so as to get a better evaluation. SWOT asks four simple questions in an elaborate way. The first two— what are your Organization's strength and weaknesses? It helps to assess your organization internally. The second two— what opportunities does your organization have and what potential threats does it face?—assess your organization's position within its environment. Of these four questions, two look at helpful areas (strengths and opportunities) and two address harmful areas. It is useful to ask these four questions with respect to both the overall business model and each of its nine Building Blocks. This type of SWOT analysis provides a good basis for further discussions, decision-making, and ultimately innovation around business models.

SWOT Analysis can be used to "kick off" strategy formulation, or in a more sophisticated way as a serious strategy tool. You can also use it to get an understanding of your competitors, which can give you the insights you need to craft a coherent and successful competitive position. When carrying out your SWOT Analysis, be realistic and rigorous. Apply it at the right level, and supplement it with other option-generation tools where appropriate.

SWOT Questionnaire –

Instructions:
Please fill the table with values that you are certain of, at least as accurately as possible good points. Read each individual instruction

Let's, Start with **Strengths:**
Where 1 denotes the lowest or bad points while 5 denotes good points or simply that your organization completely complies with the mentioned factor.

Factors to consider	Points Awarded				
Score	1	2	3	4	5
Advantages of proposition					
Capabilities					
Competitive advantages					
USP's (unique selling points)					
Resources, People					
Experience					
knowledge, data					
Financial reserves					
likely returns					
Marketing - reach, awareness					
distribution					
Innovative aspects					
Location and geographical consideration					
Pricing					
quality					
Accreditations, qualifications, certifications					

systems, IT, communications					
Cultural, attitudinal, behavioral					
`Management cover					
Sum of all the above factors =					

Now, moving on to **weaknesses:** Here, mark 1 if your company has very little compliance with the said statement or negates it, Example suppose your proposition is very advantageous then mark 1 at the first question. Similarly for the vice-versa.

Factors to consider	Points awarded				
Score	1	2	3	4	5
Disadvantages of proposition					
Gaps in capabilities					
Lack of competitive strength					
Reputation, presence and reach					
Financials					
Own known vulnerabilities					

Timescales					
deadlines and pressures					
Cash flow, start-up cash-drain					
Continuity, supply chain robustness					
Effects on core activities distractions					
Reliability of data, plan predictability					
Morale, commitment					
Leadership, Accreditations					
Processes and systems					
Management cover					
Sum of all the above factors =					

Now, moving on to **Opportunity:** The list contains a set of factors that can be considered as opportunity under the right set of circumstances. Here, if an opportunity seems definitely possible mark 5 else mark a lower value depending on its feasibility.

Factors to consider	Points awarded				
	1	2	3	4	5
Market developments					
Competitors' vulnerabilities					
Industry or lifestyle trends					
Technology development					
Innovation					
Global influences					
New markets					
Niche target markets					
Geographical import					
Geographical export					
New USP's					
Tactics - surprise, major contracts					
Business and product development					
Information and research					
Partnerships, agencies, distribution					
Volumes, production					
Economy					

Seasonal influences					
Sum of all of the above =					

Lastly, now moving to **Threat:** The below given factors can be rated as 1 if the factor is not seen much as a threat and 5 if the factor is an immediate threat.

Factors to consider	Points awarded				
	1	2	3	4	5
Political effects					
Legislative effects					
Environmental effects					
IT developments					
Competitor plans					
Market demand					
New technologies, services, ideas					
Vital contracts and partners					
Sustaining internal capabilities					
Obstacles faced					

Insurmountable weaknesses					
Loss of key staff					
Sustainable financial backing					
Economy - home, abroad					
Seasonality effects					
Sum of all of the above =					

The aforementioned SWOT has been made on a general level, you can customize yours to suite your specific start up. The only key is that the sum of strengths and opportunities should be maximum, while that of weaknesses and threats should be minimum.

Rome wasn't built in a day and so are successful startups they require utmost dedication and relentless efforts. What best way to show the credibility of the above statements than to prove it. In the next chapter that follows, a few success stories are mentioned mostly of those startups whose examples have been used in the above chapters. Some of you might have known or read about a few of these persons and their journeys before, yet there is a lot that you can grasp from the pages following

Chapter 5: Inspirational Stories

Reliance Industries- Dhirubhai Ambani

Was founded by Dhirajlal Hirachand Ambani (28 December 1932 – 6 July 2002), better known as Dhirubhai Ambani, was an Indian business tycoon. Ambani took Reliance Industries public in 1977, and by 2007 the combined fortune of the family was $60 billion, making the Ambanis the second richest family in the world. Ambani died on 6 July 2002. Ambani started with 1000 rupee in his hand and earned money by working with a firm in Yemen in the 1950s and moved to Mumbai in 1958 to start his own business in spices. After making modest profits, he moved into textiles and opened a mill in Ahmedabad. He founded Reliance Industries in 1966, and as of 2014, the company has over 100,000 employees and provides almost 5% of the Central Government's total tax revenue. As of 2014, Reliance Industries was listed among top Fortune 500 list of world's biggest companies by revenues.

Dhirubhai Ambani returned from Yemen to India and started "Majin" in partnership with Champaklal Damani, his second cousin, who lived with him in Aden, Yemen. Majin was to import polyester yarn and export spices to Yemen. The first office of the Reliance Commercial Corporation was a 350 sq ft (33 m^2) room with a telephone, one table and three chairs. Initially, they had two assistants to help them with their business. During this period, Ambani and his family stayed in a two-bedroom apartment at the Jai Hind Estate in Bhuleshwar, Mumbai. In 1965, Champaklal Damani and Dhirubhai Ambani ended their partnership and Ambani started on his own. It is believed that both had different temperaments and a different take on how to conduct business. While Damani was a cautious trader and did not believe in building yarn inventories, Ambani was a known risk-taker and believed in building inventories, anticipating a price rise, and make lots of profit.

Many questions were raised by his detractors and the press. Not many people were able to understand as to how a yarn trader until a few years ago was able to get in such a huge amount of cash flow during a crisis period. The answer to this was provided by the then finance minister and now President, Pranab Mukherjee in the Parliament. He informed the house that a Non-Resident Indian had invested up to ₹ 220 million in Reliance during 1982-83. These investments were routed through many companies like Crocodile, Lota and Fiasco. These companies were primarily registered in Isle of Man. The interesting factor was that all the promoters or owners of these companies had a common surname Shah. An investigation by the Reserve Bank of India in the incident did not find any unethical or illegal acts or transactions committed by Reliance or its promoters.

Dhirubhai Ambani was admitted to the Breach Candy Hospital in Mumbai on 24 June 2002 after he suffered a major stroke. It was his second stroke, the first one had occurred in February 1986 and had paralyzed his right hand. He was in a coma for more than a week and a number of doctors were consulted. He died on 6 July 2002.

"The country has lost iconic proof of what an ordinary Indian fired by the spirit of enterprise and driven by determination can achieve in his own lifetime"- Atal Bihari Vajpayee, *Former Prime Minister of India*

Tata group of companies- Ratan Tata

Ratan Naval Tata, one of the greatest Indian businessmen of India, was born on 28th Dec, 1940, was the chairman of Tata group from 1991 to 2012. Named after his grandfather, he was brought up and raised by his grandmother as his parents were separated when he was just seven years old. Ratan did good schooling from reputed schools and then acquired a management degree from Harvard Business School in 1975.

Ratan Tata was always interested in cars since his childhood days. He started his career in the year 1960 in the Tata Group. He worked as a general worker in the Tata Steel. J.R.D Tata resigned from his chairmanship of Tata Group and made Rata Tata as his successor in 1991.This decision was criticized by many as Ratan Tata was not sufficiently experienced at that time. But with his impeccable leadership skills, Tata Group reached new heights to become a global brand across the world.

The group acquired many big brands under his leadership such as Tetley, Jaguar, Land Rover, Corus, etc. Tata consultancy services was built under the vision of his leadership. The launch of Tata Nano and Tata Indica was a direct result out of his interests in cars from childhood. Tata Nano is the cheapest car in the world. Ratan Tata resigned from all his responsibilities in the year 2012. He resigned on his 75th birthday and his responsibilities were transferred to Cyrus Mistry, son of Palonji Mistry and M.D of Shapoorji Pallonji Group.

Ratan Tata is currently chairing Emeritus of Tata Sons. He also continues to serve as a chairman of some of the major trusts of Tata Group. He has also been a member of the Prime Minister's Council in Trade and Industry. Rata Tata is also a director on the board of Alcoa Inc.

Ratan Tata is a renowned personality and received many awards and recognitions across the world. He received the prestigious honorary Padma Vibhushan in the year 2008. He also received the Padma

Bhushan in the year 2000 for his tremendous work done throughout his life building the Tata Empire. He received the Honorary Doctor of Laws by York University, Canada in 2014.Some of the other notable awards received globally are Foreign Associate by National Academy of Engineering, Sayaji Ratna Award by Baroda Management Association, Hadrian Award by World Monument Fund, Honorary Doctorate by University of Amsterdam, Inspired Leadership Award by The Performance Theatre, Honorary Doctor of Business Administration from Ohio State University. These awards are just to name a few.

Though Ratan Tata was judged earlier to have risen because of his surname, world saw through his excellent vision and leadership as the Empire reached the top in the Indian Economy. A true businessman with a clear strategy, vision and commitment, Rata Tata stands as an example of true success achieved with true success achieved no matter what it takes.

Shangri La – Robert Kuok

One of the most successful tycoons who rule the business-world, Robert Kuok, the Malaysian billionaire, is a living legend. No one would perhaps have had as many businesses as him, all of them so big. Robert Kuok, 91, had tried his hand in sugar-cane, oil, mining, flour, hotels, publishing and animal feed businesses, striking a huge success in whatever he touched.
Kuok's story is one of those inspiring rags-to-riches saga. His up-hill climb started as an office-boy, after which he became the clerk of a rice trading department in Singapore. Robert Kuok however, was a quick learner. Three years in the rice trading department helped him learn the trading business. He later began back the same in his home town of Johor along with his brothers and a cousin.

Shortly after that, he founded the Malayan sugar manufacturing co, which quickly gained popularity. It went on to become a monopoly in sugar production space of

Malaysia producing 80% of Malaysia's sugar and 10% of world's sugar. That's precisely how Kuok got his nick name, '**the sugar king of Asia**'. Establishing monopoly was not easy. "Have you ever seen Michael Jordan play when he's on a rhythm run? It was exactly like that" Kuok says modestly.

Naturally, this ambitious and immensely clever businessman did not just stop at that. He started a chain of hotels, the famous 'Shangri-la' which is now spread out through the world and is all set to open its 71st hotel.
The 91 year old now has a lot of investments in huge businesses in nearly all of the Asian countries, Indonesia, Australia, Malaysia, and Singapore, Philippines, Indonesia and lot of other non-Asian countries. With so many businesses in so many countries, this incredible business man believes that he is the "little string that ties the rings together"

Experts would often say that his speed and cleverness led to that near-impossible success. Also, the man, they say, was never afraid to collaborate with the rest of the world unlike the eastern businessmen of the early 20th century and that was one more thing that led to him being one of the most successful businessmen of the east.

As per the Forbes list, Robert Kuok was declared the Richest Man of Malaysia and the Second Richest in South East Asia. In the Forbes' list of the richest men of 2013, he was ranked at 76th place.
Kuok, who is now retired, will always be revered as one of the foremost eastern business men who gave birth to multinational business ventures for Malaysia and the world. His talent in business is unparalleled and his story continues to awe and inspire a lot of businessmen throughout the globe.

Alibaba – Jack Ma

Jack Ma is the kind of exceptional and talented leaders who redefine the path of success. Defying the odds Jack Ma spearheaded e-commerce in China. As the Executive Chairman and founder of Alibaba Group, China's leading Internet business entity, he is among the topmost Chinese entrepreneurs, who made it to the coveted Forbes list in recent years. Jack Ma deviated from conventional methods to give his country the benefits of Internet based commerce. He lacked any technology and computing background and that makes his success even more astounding than the likes of Mark Zuckerberg and Bill Gates. When he started his career as an English teacher, few could have predicted him to become an internet mogul.

Jack Ma was born and raised in Hangzhou, in China's Zhejiang Province. His zeal to enhance his aptitude and acquire new skills was evident from childhood. As a teenager, he started communicating with foreign tourists to enhance his English skills. He entered the Hangzhou Normal University and completed graduation in English. Later in his life he attended Cheung Kong Graduate School of Business in Beijing. He forayed into website making when the concept was in its infancy in China. In 1995, he started an online business when computers had not yet become a household item in China. Despite being deemed risky, his determination was unaffected. Thus China Pages, possibly the first officially registered web business of China was set up.

The Yellow Pages website was not a resounding success, prompting Jack Ma to join the commerce ministry for a period. After shifting back to Hangzhou, in 1999 he set up Alibaba as a B2B marketplace site. Alibaba.com enabled Chinese exporters to connect with overseas buyers. Ma managed to attract Softbank and Goldman Sachs as investors later. After consolidating the position of Alibaba, Ma shifted focus to consumer-to-consumer platform. Taobao was formed in 2003. His strategy to keep it free affected the profits and drew widespread criticism, but Ma was unruffled. Taobao gained a majority of market share in two years. The courage to take on an established giant like eBay and emerge a winner is no mean feat.

Alibaba group has diversified into nine major subsidiaries- including Alipay and Alibaba Cloud Computing. Alibaba ventured into the state-dominated and staid industries in China including finance and retail. Ma is now venturing into film production.
A visionary, Jack Ma is an inspiration to an entire generation.

Dalian Wanda Group-Wang Jianlin

"Never start a business just to make money. Start a business to make difference". This quote best applies to the Chinese business tycoon Wang Jianlin. Known as "The Wealthiest person in China", he never started business with a motive of quick money during that point of time. The real estate honcho was more interested in longevity.

Wang Jianlin says that "Great companies are born, not developed, because each company has its own DNA" and that is absolutely true in his case.

Owner of "Dalian Wanda Group" which is one of the largest and best real estate developers, Jianlin purchased AMC Entertainment for $2.6 billion in 2013. His secret is rather straight to the point – it is pretty easy to achieve results with simple tricks than with complicated ones.

The beginnings for this visionary were very humble. Wang started his career with the People's Liberation Army from 1970 to 1986. In 1986, he worked as Office administrator for Xigang District in Dalian City. Later in the year, he became the General Manager of Xigang Residential Development Company.

Wang Jianlin started Dalian Wanda Group with mere $130,000. The company now has grown into a huge enterprise. His start up is currently a conglomerate of five different areas – Luxury hotels, a Chinese departmental store chain, commercial property, cultural industry and tourism. He has assets in more than 60 cities in China. His complete business comprises of forty departmental stores, forty six departmental stores and each one has 10,000 employees. Dalian Wanda Group runs around 25 five star hotels and is in partnership with hotels like Accor, Hilton and Starwood. The group flauntsworld's largest theater with 700+ screens which includes 440+ IMAX screens. Wang Jianlin had tough time in the year 1993, when government stopped providing loans to the real estate firms, asking to pay back all the pending loans rolled out so far. Jianlin faced a lot of pressure at this moment and was even hospitalized for around one week. But he had learned something new with the experience that led him to establish a Global Empire.

An eldest among 5 brothers, Wang is married to Lin Ning. The couple has two sons and one daughter. In 2013, he was ranked as 128th Wealthiest Person in the World by Forbes. The same year, he was ranked as the Wealthiest Person in China by Bloomberg. In the year 2014, he is ranked as the 26th Richest Person in the World by Hurun report.

Wang Jianlin proved to the world that there is no specific secret for success.

Winning comes from preparation, learning from failures and hard work. According to him, a business which is just for making money is a poor business.

Jianlin's Mantra for success - "Any business should aim for longevity".

Samsung - Lee Kun-Hee

By far the Richest Man in South Korea, Lee Kun-Hee serves as the chairman of the huge electronics empire, the Samsung Group. Lee's father, Lee Byung-Chul, set up Samsung in 1938. In Korean, Samsung means "three stars."
Back then, the firm used to export vegetables, fruit, and dried fish to Manchuria and Beijing. When Byung-Chul died in 1987, Lee took over control of the company. Lee joined Samsung in 1968 and within 2 weeks of his father's demise, he appointed himself as chairman.
Interestingly, Lee is Byung-Chul's third son. Armed with a Degree in Economics from Waseda University and an MBA from George Washington University, Lee brought about a total transformation in Samsung. Previously, it was known as a budget company. Lee changed all of that to make Samsung an internationally renowned firm. It can be argued that Samsung is now the most prominent Asian brand in the world.

His famous 1993 quote, "Change everything except your wife and kids" summarizes his efforts in a nutshell. In the early 1990s, Samsung's corporate culture was deeply Korean and the company expended all its efforts into manufacturing cheap and low-quality products.

Lee understood the power of a diverse workforce and added foreign employees to the staff of Samsung. This helped chart the success of Samsung to the heights it has reached today.

Samsung Electronics, one of the subsidiaries of the Samsung Group, is currently the world's leading manufacturer and developer of semiconductors. In 2007, it was a part of Fortune magazine's list of 100 Largest Corporations of the World.

Lee's astounding turnaround of the company can be appreciated by the fact that the revenue of Samsung today is 39 times higher than it was in 1987. The firm alone generates approximately 20 percent of the GDP of Korea.

After Samsung was embroiled in a slush funds scandal in 2008, Lee stepped down. After being pardoned by the government of

South Korea, he returned as chairman in 2010.

Lee is married to Ra-Hee Hong, who owns a $1.5 billion stake in Samsung. His son, Lee Jae-yong serves as the vice-chairman of Samsung Electronics. His elder daughter, Lee Boo-jin is the CEO of Hotel Shilla, a luxury chain of hotels. His younger daughter, Lee Seo-Hyun, is the president of Samsung Everland, which is the main holding company for the Samsung Group. Personally, Lee has been through a harrowing time and is currently in an uncertain medical condition. In 2005, he was diagnosed with lung cancer. He was also suffering from respiratory infections and pneumonia for a long time.

Adani Group – Gautam Adani

This entrepreneur has taken his family business and his own Adani group to new heights and today helps contribute to the growth of Indian economy and infrastructure. Adani group is today a key player in businesses ranging from coal mining and trading, exploration for gas and oil to ports and power generation. Adani group is one of the biggest port operators in the country.

Gautam Adani was born into family which had textile business. However, family business did not interest him as much and he moved to Mumbai at the age of 18 and made his first million as a diamond broker in his third year in Mumbai. At 20, he was a millionaire. But he headed back to Ahmedabad on his brother's behest and started working with dealings in PVC Gautam Adani went on to establish the Adani group in 1988 and started with dealings in agricultural commodities and power. Luck and changes in economy worked in his favor and the liberalization and economic reforms of 1991 helped push the growth of the business and increased revenues and profits for his company. From there on, there was no turning back and the business grew to new heights, with increased diversification into all kinds of business and industries.

Adani group has a widespread portfolio and business undertakings. Gautam Adani, at the helm of the successful conglomerate, is known for his risk appetite and his eye for businesses that he takes to new heights and turn into profitable undertakings. He works closely with his people and teams to drive them to perfection, and successful execution of business ideas and undertakings. Gautam has been exposed to a lot of controversy of late owing to land dealings for his business which have not been properly sanctioned. Also, many of his business's industrial units have no proper clearance from the environment authority of the state and hence have been a point of wrath for the high Court of state of Gujarat. In spite of the many controversies that Adani may be linked with, this business tycoon leaves no stone unturned in pushing his company higher up the ladder. In a recent dealing, Adani elbowed Sajjan Jindal and acquired the famed Udupi Thermal Power Plant at a whopping 6,000-crore rupees. It is said that Gautam Adani sealed the deal in a negotiation that lasted merely 100 hours!

The Adani group is involved in a lot of philanthropic work and gives back to the society as a part of Adani's personal commitment and also a part of their social responsibility as a corporate. The Adani foundation works across many states and the philanthropic undertakings of the groups that are headed by Gautam's wife. They are operational in close to six states in the country, setting up schools for education, promoting community health and growth, development of rural areas and helping people learn skills to earn and maintain livelihood.

Gautam Adani is a perfect example of business genius merged with perseverant visionary.

Sun Pharmaceuticals – Dilip Shanghvi

There are several Pharmaceutical majors based in India, but few have been able to match or replicate the steady rise and growth of Sun Pharmaceutical Industries Limited. The man behind its unmatched success is Dilip Shanghvi, the former Chairman of the company which is now the leading drug maker in India.

As of now, he is the third richest person of India and 7th top wealthiest and self-made billionaire in Asia. When he started Sun Pharmaceutical Industries in 1983, hardly anyone could assume the stupendous success he will achieve.

Dilip Shanghvi has not played safe to reach the zenith of success in his illustrious career and he has taken some unconventional steps to take Sun Pharmaceutical Industries to the number one spot. He also serves as the MD and Chairman of Sun Pharmaceutical Advanced Research Company, the first ever pure-R&D Company enlisted with Indian stock exchanges. He made headlines by making the move to acquire trouble ridden drug maker Ranbaxy and enhancing company revenues significantly.

It is quite hard to believe that the third richest person in India started his pharmaceutical company with just five products and five people. He had an even humbler beginning and started as a pharmaceutical products wholesaler in Kolkata. Dilip Shanghvi has succeeded in the industry by deciding to stress on niche markets like lifestyle and psychiatry drugs. The company's revenue has grown fourfold and it now stands at a staggering Rs 22.37 billion.

The first unit of Sun Pharmaceuticals was set up in Gujarat to manufacture psychiatry medications. Dilip Shanghvi had a talent for turning around companies in distress. He has been consistent and balanced in his expansion plans and implementation. His takeover of Caraco Pharma, which took place in 1997 was not seen as a worthy move by many industry experts. Through his efforts the loss-making company is now making money.

Each of his acquisitions was well planned and they enabled him to diversify business to new sectors. The takeover of Milmet Labs enabled Sun to venture into ophthalmology. In 1987, when the company began selling products on a national scale, it was ranked 108th. Now, it sits at number six, which is nothing short of phenomenal.

Under the leadership of Dilip Shanghvi, Sun Pharmaceuticals continued its expansion and joint ventures with several European and US drug majors. 2012 was a significant year when the company acquired two US companies, URL Pharma Inc. and DUSA Pharmaceuticals Inc. However, the acquisition of Israel-based Taro made Sun a big player in overseas market and helped Dilip Shanghvi redefine success in the sector. With Taro acquisition, Sun can tap the customer potential in Canada along with other foreign markets. An even bigger deal was his decision to acquire troubled Indian rival Ranbaxy Laboratories from Japan's Daiichi Sankyo this year. While this move made some industry veterans frown, later the majority agreed about the viability of the landmark deal.

Dilip Shanghvi has ambitious plans chalked out both for Indian and overseas market. For Dilip Shanghvi and his company, the Ranbaxy takeover can prove to be a big game-changer. It will give him the scope to spread into emerging markets where Ranbaxy products are popular. He looks forward to use his skill at turning around weak businesses and revive Ranbaxy.

While the United States remains a large source of Sun's revenue, it has enough expansion scopes there. Sanghvi is now focusing on specific product niches to carry forward the growth of Sun Pharmaceuticals. Apart from focusing on dermatology drugs, his company will also concentrate on enhancing business in Europe.

Soft Bank - Masayoshi Son

Masayoshi Son is the Founder and CEO of the telecommunications firm Softbank. After establishing Softbank, Son went on to work with top organizations like Yahoo (CEO, Yahoo Japan) and BB Technologies (Chairman of the Board). He currently heads Sprint Corporation Mobile and Telecom sector. According to Forbes 2014 survey, Masayoshi Son is the Richest Man in Japan.

Masyoshi Son was born in Tosu, Japan on August 11, 1957. Although belonging to Korean ethnicity, his family adopted Japanese culture and the surname Yasumoto. He graduated from University of California in Economics. Even as a child, Son showed great interest in computer chips. As he grew, Son was convinced that computers would soon revolutionize the commercial sector. After completing his graduation, Son founded Softbank Corporation in 1981 as an internet and telecommunications organization. In 1986, he became the Chairman and CEO of Softbank

Corporation. In early 2000, he joined Yahoo Japan, where he led the company as President and CEO. After this, he joined BB Technologies Corporation, which is now known as the Softbank BB Corporation

Son had established Yahoo BB in 2001. In 2006, Vodafone sold its mobile division to Softbank for 1.75 trillion Japanese Yen. Soon after the acquisition of Vodafone though, Softbank was in crisis. Yahoo BB still managed to acquire Japan Telecom and clear some of the dues of Softbank. Today Yahoo BB leads the Japan's broadband networking under the guidance of Masayoshi Son. Son bought 76 per cent of Sprint Corporation soon after joining the company. He is now the chairman of Sprint. Massayoshi Son's Softbank has acquired some of the most influential organizations. It now has an established reputation worldwide in telecom sector. Recently, the company started piling up stakes of Supercell (Finland) and Brightstar (US).

Masayoshi Son is an active philanthropist. He has played an integral part in the recovery strategy during the Fukushima Daiichi nuclear disaster in 2011. He was also instrumental in establishing solar power projects in Japan. In 2011, Son donated $120 million to help the victims of Tohoku Tsunami.

Masayoshi Son, with a net worth of $19.7 Billion, as of April 2014, is reportedly the Richest man in Japan and one among the top 10 richest globally. Additionally, he is listed as one of the notable influential people of his time.

A forward thinking entrepreneur, Masayoshi Son mastered the art of taking calculated risks that pay off in the end. His step by step methodology in establishing and planning business stands as a fine learning for aspiring young entrepreneurs all over the world.

Miyake Design Studio – Issey Misake

Critically acclaimed and mega-popular Japanese fashion designer Issey Miyake certainly hasn't had the easiest of lives. Born in Hiroshima, Japan, on the 22nd of April 1938, he grew up to see his home destroyed during the Allied bombing of Hiroshima during World War II. Miyake survived the blast, and continued his schooling as his hometown was gradually rebuilt after the war.

That experience forged a remarkably distaste for violence in Miyake, one that was cemented after his mother died three years later due to radiation poisoning from the bombing. Miyake soon moved to Tokyo to begin studying graphic design, building his passion for innovative, technology-inspired fashion during the same time period.

After graduation, he moved abroad, working for the industry's biggest names in cities like Paris and New York. Miyake was a good assistant to many of fashion's at-the-time biggest icons, working as a relatively introspective outsider while picking up the skills of the trade. In 1970, after helping others for six years, he returned to Japan seeking a more ambitious opportunity in the fashion world.

Thanks to his determination and focus, it happened. In 1970, Miyake founded the Miyake Design Studio, a specialist female fashion design studio. The studio's innovative designs picked up a great deal of praise in Japan's growing fashion scene, and Miyake's company was soon producing a wide range of items for women both in Japan and based outside of the country.

Unlike other fashion designers, Miyake had little interest in the ostentatious, flamboyant designs of the European labels. He instead preferred to look at how the world was changing – how technology was shaping the culture around him – and implement its developments into his work. Known as the fashion designer's only great technologist, his work is inspired by both machinery and electronica.

This innovation in design soon turned into an innovation in production, and Miyake's company took an active role in developing a new system of pleating. Allowing for garments to be produced with a much greater level of quality and turned it into one of the key developments in fashion throughout the late 1980s and 1990s.

While Miyake's reputation as a fashion designer is unquestioned, he's perhaps more famous among young people due to his interesting friendships. A close friend of Lucie Rie, he adapted her famous pottery work into the inspiration for an entire set of high-end dresses, using the symmetry and style of classic pottery to craft beautiful garments.

Likewise, he was a close friend of Apple Inc. cofounder Steve Jobs, and was known for designing the world famous black turtle necks that Jobs wore on a daily basis. After Jobs requested a custom fitted turtleneck to wear during presentations, Miyake created hundreds of them and mailed them directly to Jobs, giving him enough clothing to last him the rest of his life.

From his contributions to fashion to his importance as a public Japanese intellectual, Issey Miyake is a widely respected and influential public figure. In 2010, he was awarded the Order of Culture in his native Japan for contribution to fashion. His company continues to be one of the most successful worldwide, selling everything from garments to technology-inspired designer wristwatches.

Cheung Kong- Li Ka Shing

Li Ka Shing's early years were spent in the Coastal city of **Chiu Chow** in China. When he was a teenager, Li had fled to Hong Kong to evade war. After his father died of tuberculosis. Li dropped out of high school and found employment in a plastics trading company.

When he was 22, Li began his own business of making **plastic toys**. His first company was Cheung Kong. What started as a plastic manufacturing unit blossomed into a top real estate investment entity. In 1972, Cheung Kong Industries was listed in Hong Kong Stock Exchange

While Cheung Kong Industries was growing exponentially, in 1979 Li acquired Hutchison Whampoa Limited after a deal with HSBC. It led to the creation of a massive conglomerate with business spreading into various sectors. Later, he focused on investing in top container port facilities in many countries. Under Li's leadership and supervision, Hutchison Whampoa Limited ventured into several sectors including retail, asset treading and telecommunications. Hutchison Telecommunications sold majority of its controlling stake in Hutchison Essar in India to the Vodafone group.

Li also made a foray into the fast growing technology and internet business. Li Ka Shing Foundation bought stake in Facebook with a $120 million deal. He also invested in Spotify, a popular online music streaming service.

Despite being the Largest and Richest Entrepreneur in Asian sub content, Li finds time to focus on philanthropic activities. In 1981, he set up Shantou University. He also donated to the Hong Kong Polytechnic University in 2001 post which a tower was named after him.

He sold his stake worth $1.2 billion CAD in CIBC in 2005 and the proceeds went to Li Ka Shing Foundation.

Li's success is not just the proverbial rags to riches story but also a lesson in determination and humility.

I hope that after reading about these success stories, you are bubbling with inspiration and confidence in yourself. Now, all that's left is for you to execute what you have designed and work with perseverance toward achieving success. Hoping that you found this book quite helpful.

www.ingramcontent.com/pod-product-compliance
Lightning Source LLC
Chambersburg PA
CBHW070826180526
45168CB00002B/751